Piano - Vocal - Guitar

The Rolling Stones
Anthology

ISBN 0-7935-3648-0

HAL•LEONARD™
CORPORATION
7777 W. BLUEMOUND RD. P.O. BOX 13819 MILWAUKEE, WI 53213

The Rolling Stones Anthology

Piano - Vocal - Guitar

CONTENTS

ALL THE WAY DOWN

Words and Music by MICK JAGGER
and KEITH RICHARDS

all the way (all the way) all the way, all the way down.

She went

D.S. (Verse 5) and repeat chorus till FADE

Tempo I

down down down down. Down down down down. Down down down _ Down down down. _ (5.) You

VERSE 2:
She showed me love a hundred ways,
How she pimped and how she paid.
All the daughters, all the sons,
All were welcome, all would come.

VERSE 3:
I was King, Mr Cool
Just like a snobby little fool. (Like kids are now)
I dreamed of reaching greater heights,
I raved about it every night, talk is cheap.

VERSE 5:
You give me back that time right now.
I can see it if I close my eyes.
Was every minute just a waste?
Was every hour a foolish chase?

ANGIE

Words and Music by MICK JAGGER
and KEITH RICHARDS

BEAST OF BURDEN

Words and Music by MICK JAGGER
and KEITH RICHARDS

you to make love to me._____
you to make love to me._____

Am I hard e - nough__ am I rough e - nough__ am I

rich e - nough__ I'm not too blind__ to see_____

I'll nev - er be your Beast_____ of Bur - den

BEFORE THEY MAKE ME RUN

Words and Music by MICK JAGGER
and KEITH RICHARDS

To Coda

But let me walk be - fore they make___ me
So let me walk be - fore they make___ me
I wan - na walk be - fore they make___ me

run. _____
run. _____
run. _____

Repeat and fade

DOO DOO DOO DOO DOO
(HEARTBREAKER)

Words and Music by MICK JAGGER
and KEITH RICHARDS

EMOTIONAL RESCUE

Words and Music by MICK JAGGER
and KEITH RICHARDS

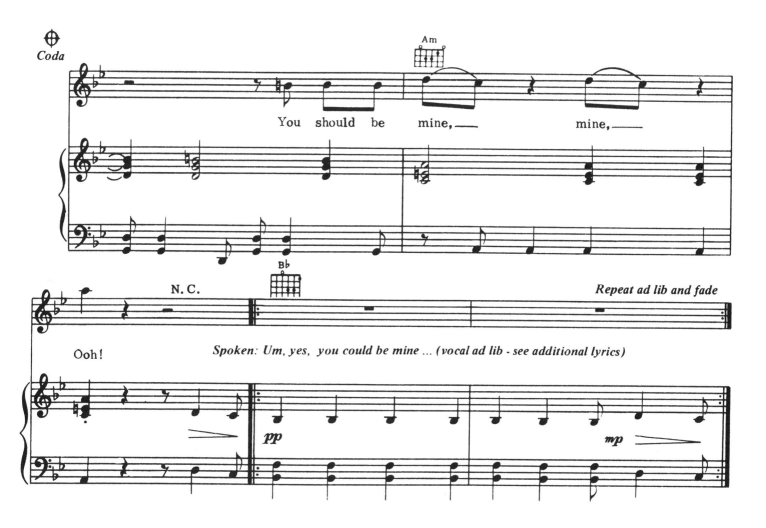

Coda

You should be mine,——— mine,———

Ooh!

Spoken: Um, yes, you could be mine ... (vocal ad lib - see additional lyrics)

Repeat ad lib and fade

Verse 2: Don't you know promises were never made to keep?
Just like the night, they dissolve in sleep.
I'll be your saviour, steadfast and true. *(To 2nd ending:)*

Bridge: 2. Yeah, I'm crying baby,
I'm like a child, baby.
3. Like a child, yeah,
So like a child, like a child, like a child, like a child.

Verse 3: You think you're one of a special breed,
You think that you're his pet Pekinese.
I'll be your saviour, steadfast and true. *(To 3rd ending:)*

Bridge: 4. Last night I was dreaming,
5. How you'd be mine, but I was crying
6. Like a child. Yeah, I was crying,
7. Crying like a child. You will be
Mine, mine, mine, mine, mine,
8. All mine. You could be mine, could be mine,
Be mine, all mine.

Verse 4: I come to you, so silent in the night,
So stealthy, so animal quiet.
I'll be your saviour, steadfast and true. *(To 4th ending:)*

Vocal
ad lib: *. . .tonight and every night. I will be your knight in shining armour*
Coming to your emotional rescue.
You will be mine, you will be mine, all mine.
You will be mine, you will be mine, all mine.
I want to be your knight in shining armour, riding across the
Desert with a fine Arab charger.
(Instr. ad lib ... (fade)

FEEL ON BABY

Words and Music by MICK JAGGER
and KEITH RICHARDS

VERSE 2:
From the first time, such a crush;
Such excitement, such a rush.
In the kitchen; in the car;
In the ditch. On the dirty floor.

VERSE 3:
Wanderlust and love disease
Taken over and strangled me.
Cure my body, make me whole.
Feed my body, feed my soul.

FOOL TO CRY

Words and Music by MICK JAGGER
and KEITH RICHARDS

Vocal Ad Lib

I'm a fool, baby,
I'm a fool, baby,
I'm a certified fool, now
I want to tell ya,
Gotta tell ya, baby,
I'm a fool, baby,
Certified fool for ya, mama, come on,
I'm a fool, I'm a fool,
I'm a fool.

FARAWAY EYES

Words and Music by MICK JAGGER
and KEITH RICHARDS

1. I __ was __ driving __ home, __ early __ Sunday __ morning __ through __
2. I __ had __ an __ arrangement __ to __ meet __ a __ girl, __ and __ I __ was __ kind __ of __ late, __ And __
3. Well __ the __ preacher __ kept __ right __ on __ saying __ that __ all __ I __ had __ to __ do __ was __

HANG FIRE

Words and Music by MICK JAGGER
and KEITH RICHARDS

IT MUST BE HELL

Words and Music by MICK JAGGER
and KEITH RICHARDS

dark-ness still a-bides.___ Must Be Hell___

Sing cue notes after 3rd & 4th verses:
CHORUS

liv-ing in the world, liv-ing in the world like you. Must Be

Hell

liv-ing in the world, liv-ing in the world like

To Coda ◆

you.

VERSE 3:
Keep in a straight line. Stay in tune.
No need to worry, 'cause only fools
End up in prison or concience cells,
Or in asylums they help to build.

VERSE 4:
We're free to worship; we're free to speak.
We're free to kill — that's guaranteed.
We got our problems, that's for sure.
Clean up the backyard; don't lock the door.

IT'S ONLY ROCK 'N' ROLL (BUT I LIKE IT)

Words and Music by MICK JAGGER
and KEITH RICHARDS

MISS YOU

Words and Music by MICK JAGGER
and KEITH RICHARDS

Steady Beat

I've been hold-ing out so long,— I've been sleep-ing all a-lone,— Lord I

miss you,— I've been hang-ing on the phone, I've been

ha ha ha ha___ ha ha ha ha ha___ ha___ ha ha ha ha___

Ha ha

(Solo voice) Oh!
(Group) Ooh___

ev - 'ry bod - y waits so long, ___ Oh!
Ooh___

ba - by why you wait so long, ___ Won't you come on! come on!

LIES

Words and Music by MICK JAGGER
and KEITH RICHARDS

PRETTY BEAT UP

Words and Music by MICK JAGGER,
KEITH RICHARDS and RON WOOD

VERSE 3
Yea, I'm just like a battered baby
Just left on the street. Pretty beat up.
You ought to see the state. Pretty beat up.
I've been cut with a razor. Pretty beat up.
Don't you cut me up. Don't you cut me up.
I'm pretty beat up. Pretty beat up.
Pretty beat up. Pretty beat up. *(etc..)*

RESPECTABLE

Words and Music by MICK JAGGER
and KEITH RICHARDS

Medium Rock

Well now we're res-pec-ted in so-ci-e-ty,___ you ain't wor-
now you're a pil-lar of so-ci-e-ty,___you're not wor-

-ried 'bout the things that used to be.___ We're talk-ing___
-ried 'bout the things that used to be.___ You're a rag___

SHE WAS HOT

Words and Music by MICK JAGGER
and KEITH RICHARDS

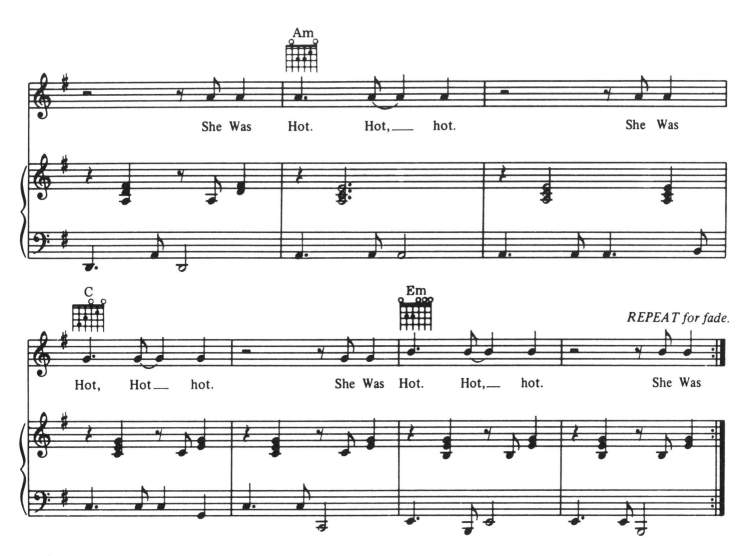

VERSE 2:
Detroit was smoky grey,
Nothing like the good old days.
I got a fever that I'm fighting.
I don't need your company,
Leave me in my misery,
I can take the rebound
Just like lightning.
And she was hot – in a 50's dress,
She was hot – her lips were flashing red,
I was lost – in her burning flesh,
I was hot – I was dripping sweat,
She was hot – in the Detroit snow,
She was hot – she had no place to go,
She was hot – on a cold and rainy night.

VERSE 3: (½ verse:- instrumental ad lib)
And she was hot – and I had the blues,
She was hot – honey where were you?
If you were in my shoes
You would be excused.
She was hot – you can never wait,
She was hot – never hesitate,
She was hot – on a cold and rainy night.

VERSE 4:
I think I'm going off the rails
Riding down the pleasure trails,
So take your passion where you find it.
Honey when you were young and fresh,
And you need the touch of your flesh,
Go take the treasure where you find it.
And she was hot – in the melted snow,
She was hot – in the molten glow,
She was hot – she got it in the blood,
She was hot – like the dam that's burst,
She was strong – she was strong and true,
She was black – and her eyes were blue,
She was lost – and she took a chance.

(CODA)

SHE'S SO COLD

Words and Music by MICK JAGGER
and KEITH RICHARDS

Lively Rock 'N' Roll Beat

1. I'm so hot for her, I'm so hot for her,
2. tried re-wir-ing her, tried re-fir-ing her, I

I'm so hot for her, and she's so cold. I'm so hot for her,
think her en-gine is per-ma-nent-ly stalled. She's so cold, she's so

I'm so hot for you, I'm so hot for you, I'm so hot for you, and

you're so cold. I'm the burn- ing bush, I'm the burn- ing fire,

Repeat and fade
(ad lib guitar solo on repeat)

I'm the bleed- ing vol - ca - no.

START ME UP

Words and Music by MICK JAGGER
and KEITH RICHARDS

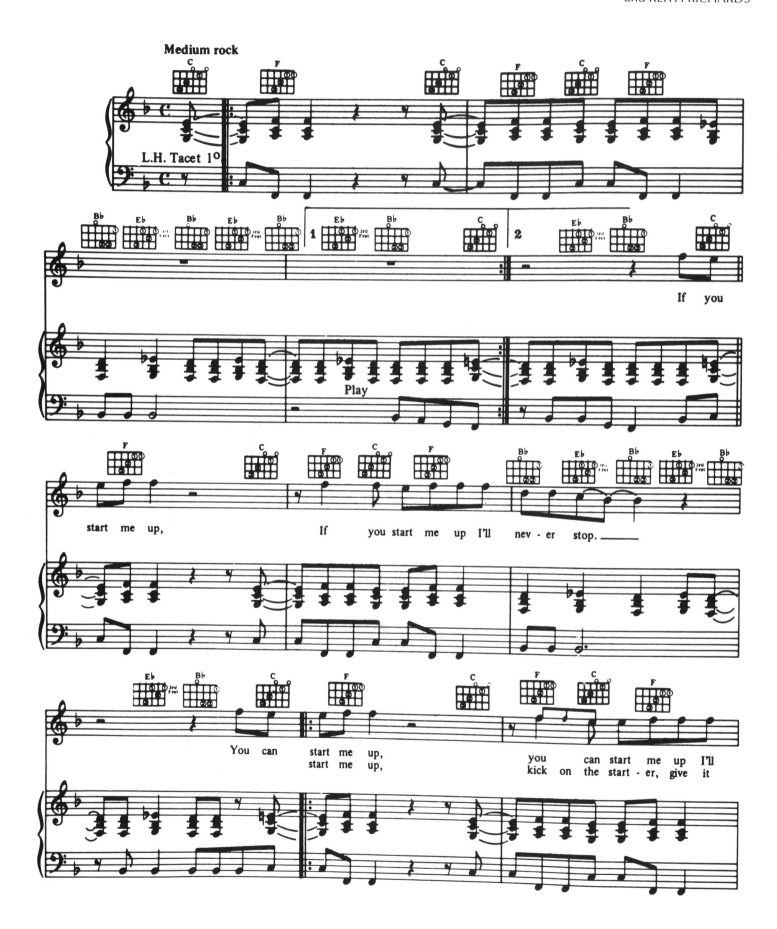

SOME GIRLS

Words and Music by MICK JAGGER
and KEITH RICHARDS

Slow Rock Beat

1. Some girls give me mon-ey,_____
5. French girls they want Car-ti-er,_____ I

some girls give me clothes;_____ some girls give me jewel-'ry_____ that I'd
-ta-li-an girls want cars;_____ A-me-ri-can girls want ev-'ry-thing in the world you could

TOO MUCH BLOOD

Words and Music by MICK JAGGER
and KEITH RICHARDS

Ev-'ry-thing you see__ on the mo-vie screen is tame.

C#m
(Spoken)

Repeat till end of
Spoken Lyric.

1st Rap
A friend of mine was this Japanese, he had a girlfriend in Paris. He tried to date her, in six months and eventually she said yes. You know he took her to his apartment, cut off her head. Put the rest of her body in the refrigerator, ate her piece by piece. Put her in the refrigerator, put her in the freezer. And when he ate her and took her bones to the Bois de Boulogne. By chance, a taxi driver noticed him burying the bones. You don't believe me; truth is stranger than fiction. We drive through there every day.

on (D.%.) 2nd Rap
Did you ever see the "Texas Chain Saw Massacre?" Horrible, wasn't it. You know, people ask me, "is it really true where you live in Texas, is that really true what they do around there, people?" I say, "yea, every time I drive through the crossroads I get scared. There's a bloke running round with a fucking chain saw. Oh! Oh! No, gonna... Oh no. Don't saw off me leg, don't saw off me arm."
When I go to the movies, you know, I would like to see something more romantic you know, like "An Officer and a Gentleman" or something. Something you can take the wife to, you know? Do you know what I mean?

Last time ———— **D.%.(Twice)**
al Coda ✛

✛ **CODA**
C#m

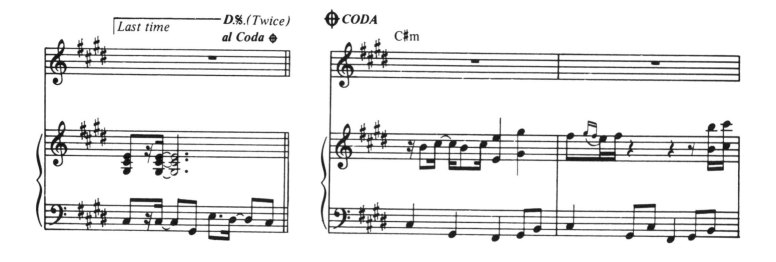

TIE YOU UP (THE PAIN OF LOVE)

Words and Music by MICK JAGGER
and KEITH RICHARDS

The Pain___ Of Love.   Yeah, that's what they   call_ it.

FINE

VERSE 2:
You dream of it passionate,
You even get a rise from it,
Feel the hot cum
Dripping on your thigh from it.
Why so divine
The pain of love?
Sometimes you crave for it,
Cry for it,
Women will die for it.
Looking back,
Cut the crap,
Was it really worth the rap?
It's hard to survive the pain of love.

VERSE 3:
No release from the jail
No parole, no bail.
Hard labour, fifty lashes.
Hard labour, money crashes.
It's hard to survive the pain of love.
The old maid is rouging up, applying the final touches,
Even though she's late for the dance.
I'll tell you tonight she's really gonna have a ball.
She's gonna really tie me up,
She's gonna really tie me up.

TOO TOUGH

Words and Music by MICK JAGGER
and KEITH RICHARDS

Medium tempo

VERSES 1, 2, 3 & 4.

1. If you want to wreck __ my life _____ Go a-head __ my love. __
2. _____
3. __ *(see additional lyrics)* _____
4. _____

Tried it once with poi-son   Tried it once with drugs __

To Coda

My cir-cu-la-tion's run-ning dry __   It's you   that drank me up. __

120

VERSE 2:

Saw you on T.V. last night in a re-run soap.
You were young and beautiful, already without hope.
But I don't think you ever knew what you've bitten off.
But in the end you spat me out, you could not chew me up.

VERSE 3:

I was married yesterday to a teenage bride.
You said it's only physical, but I love her deep inside.
I still see you in my dreams with a kitchen knife,
With it poised above your head, now who you gonna slice?

VERSE 4:

I don't think you'll ever know what you've bitten off.
But in the end you spat me out, you could not chew me up.

TUMBLING DICE

Words and Music by MICK JAGGER
and KEITH RICHARDS

UNDERCOVER (OF THE NIGHT)

Words and Music by MICK JAGGER
and KEITH RICHARDS

1. Heard the screams of Cen-tre For-ty -Two: loud e - nough to burst your brains out.
(2.3.4. *see additional lyrics*) _____

(1.) The op-po-si - tion's tongue is ___ cut in two.___ Keep off the street 'cause you're in dan-ger.
(3. & 4.) _____

(1.) Four hun-dred thousand "dis - pa - rus", lost in the jails in South A - me-ri-ca.)
(2.3.4.) _____

D.%. (Verse 4) al Coda

CODA

Un-der-co-ver Of The Night.____

keep in-side.____

Un-der-co-ver.   Keep it all out of sight.   Un-der-co-ver Of The Night.____

Repeat for Fade

Vocal/Instrumental – Ad lib. . .

VERSE 2:

The sex police are out there on the streets
Make sure the Pass Laws are not broken.
The Race Militia is got itchy fingers
All the way from New York back to Africa.

VERSE 3:

All the young men, they've been rounded up
And sent t ocamps back in the jungle.
And people whisper: people double talk.
And once proud fathers act so humble.
All the young girls, they have got the blues.
They're heading all back to Centre Forty-Two.

VERSE 4:

Down in the bars, the girls are painted blue;
Done up in lace; done up in rubber.
The Johns are jerky G. I. Joes
On R & R from Cuba and Russia.
The smell of sex; the smell of suicide.
All these things I can't keep inside.

WAITING ON A FRIEND

Words and Music by MICK JAGGER
and KEITH RICHARDS

WANNA HOLD YOU

Words and Music by MICK JAGGER
and KEITH RICHARDS

VERSE 2:
This time it's not for fun.
That you're the only one.
What should I say to you?
I only know that this starts something tonight.

VERSE 3:
But if you let me smile.
But if you know I lie.
But after all you gave
I'll be your lover; I'll be your slave.

WHEN THE WHIP COMES DOWN

Words and Music by MICK JAGGER
and KEITH RICHARDS

whip comes down, ___

when the whip comes down, ___

when the whip comes down, ___

when the whip comes down, ___

when the

(spoken) Watch out ba - by,__

check it out, check it out, check it out, check it out, check it out, check it out, check it out, check it out,

when the whip comes down,__ when the

Repeat and fade